# Your Keys to Paradise...

## By
## Phyllis "Momma" May

PUBLISHED BY
WINGSPAN PRESS

ISBN: 0-9758997-0-8

Wingspan Publishing
P.O. Box 2372
Key West, FL 33045
To order multiple copies of this publication, call 877-312-1800

Book design: Kerry Karshna
Cover: Maria@mariabellimages.com

What does all that mean? It means:
• Don't copy the book; buy it. I'm living on a fixed retirement income, Social Security and $80/week at the B&B. I need help.
• I'm not responsible if you don't like the restaurants I've recommended.
• I'm not responsible if you don't like the businesses I suggested...I had very good intentions!
• Don't make me mad. "When Momma ain't happy, ain't nobody happy!"
• You need to listen to Momma!

Photo credit: Peter Arnow

# Acknowledgements

While I am proficient at writing Letters to the Editor, articles and have a chapter in a boring anthology about teamwork, I've never even considered writing a book. But, this just happened; a little project just grew like Topsy!

No effort at thank you would be appropriate if I didn't start with my parents, Jimmy and Hazel, who instilled in me my obsession to live in Florida. My daddy would love knowing that his granddaughter was born in Florida. They, especially he, made their goal of eventually moving from Columbus, Indiana to Florida the main objective in life. That never happened as daddy died very quickly at age 47 from melanoma. Hence, the references to 'don't forget the sunscreen'.

As we stood on the hillside at his burial in Brown County, Indiana, I heard a friend of his say, "Jimmy did everything in life he ever wanted...except move to Florida." It was then that I decided that:

• I was going to live in Florida...sooner rather than later
• I was not going to go through life talking about things I'd like to do; I would do them!

My husband and I did move to Jacksonville, Florida, in 1972. For 25 years I lived there and enjoyed it. At least Florida was on my address! But, I never felt like I was in 'real' Florida.

After retiring and divorcing (not in that order), I finally decided to move to Key West. As a child, we used to fly out of this very same Key West airport, on Q Airways, to go to Havana. Of course, that was B.C. (before Castro). We stayed at the Southernmost Motel...a place I drive by nearly every day.

No acknowledgement would be complete without recognizing my daughter, Liane...the light of my life. She humors me and she's my motivation. But, I wanted her to write a chapter for Gen XYZers or whatever they are now. She just talked about it and never did it. She hasn't learned that lesson yet.

Thanks to friends that have given input and encouragement along the way...Vicki Grant and Cristina Linley. To David

Sloan, who for such a young whippersnapper really has his act together…at least when it comes to publishing books and being entrepreneurial. (I won't mention where he DOESN'T have his act together.)

Thanks to all the guests at both Courtyard by Marriotts in Key West…especially to Pat Johnson and Noah Van Oosterhout.

Thanks to all the guests at Lightbourn Inn and Scott, Kelly and Garry for putting up with me.

Finally, to my friends at Florida Speakers Association, this never would have happened without your inspiration and knowledge. Many of you are such examples of what can be done that anyone who truly wants to do things can see, by your example, that it can be done.

It would be thoughtless to only mention FSA collectively without mentioning the person who keeps me moving toward goals. I value his opinions and his advice. He has believed in me from the beginning. Thank you, Jim Barber.

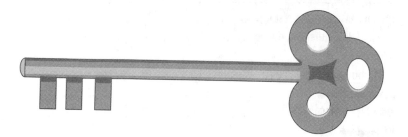

# Contents

# Introduction

Because Key West is so unique, it is often the subject of books and articles. Yet, having worked at a bed and breakfast and as a concierge at a major hotel chain, I was often asked for quick information. There is so much to tell and I finally realized that I wanted to share what I knew, without constraints.

I retired and moved to Key West in 1998. Because I was a new resident and only knew I liked the place very much, I set out to find out and become familiar with as much as possible about this quirky little town. (When you move to a tourist destination, you discover more out-of-town friends that you ever knew you had!)

After six years, this is clearly my home and I couldn't be happier. As a retiree who doesn't need a 9-5 job, I had the luxury of doing things I'd never done. My first job was as a concierge at a major hotel chain. I was in my element and felt like I was born to be a concierge! (Translate: someone who likes to tell people where to go. Merriam-Webster: Main Entry: con·cierge. Pronunciation: kOn-'syerzh. You notice the 'zh' at the end. I've looked it up. It is not kOnsyer!)

In this role, I felt personally responsible for guests having a great vacation experience. When it rained, I felt responsible! To this day, I still feel the same commitment. If I'm downtown and see people puzzling over a map, I stop to help. On several occasions I've told strangers I would take them where they wanted to go. They're amazed that someone would do that for strangers but I get satisfaction from helping them.

Let me share something with you that I learned at the hotel. Some hotels in Key West rent their concierge desk to a company. The person working there is NOT an employee of the hotel. The concierge is sometimes an employee of an attraction company. For example, the desk where I worked was "owned" by a company that provides snorkel trips. When a guest stopped by the desk and asked about snorkel trips, we had to book with that company. Personally, I preferred other snorkel trips and couldn't tell the guest that I didn't like the company I was booking them on. For that reason, I decided to write this book.

I want to be able to give suggestions without any obligation to anyone. What I put in here is strictly my personal recommendations. They are places that I usually get consistent, positive feedback about. But, there are no guarantees.

Until the book was published, no restaurant or attraction knew that they were being included. I have not, and will never, accept any money to include any business. For that reason, I hope you will assume that the information provided is here for the purpose of making your trip the best.

I am writing it in a conversational style so that you feel that we are chatting. I will be very candid. I have purposely not mentioned some attractions and restaurants. You won't find anything negative in this book about a specific place. If I haven't had a positive experience, I've simply omitted it or don't know enough to include it with confidence.

I would like your feedback. This is a work in progress and I value your opinion and input. Please use the concierge in your hotel, if you have one. Helping you, and making the commissions that go with it, provide their income. In many cases, I have provided phone numbers but it doesn't cost you more to use your concierge…it just helps that person live on this very expensive island and most people have to have more than one job. I'm not trying to take away their business but if you want help before your trip or are staying in a location without a concierge, feel free to contact me. My website is http://www.keystoparadise.info Have a wonderful visit in Paradise; I'm glad you're here!

*Logo design: Dina Designs, Int'l, Key West*

# Part I
# Coming to Key West?

# Chapter 1
# Where is it and how
# will you get here?

**C**oming to Key West? How will you get here?

## Driving?

Key West, the Florida Keys, the Conch Republic...all are references, that you will hear, to the place that many of us call 'Paradise'. Yes, the Florida Keys experience is like no other in the United States. Key West, the southernmost city in the United States, is like being on a Caribbean island without having to leave our country. It's even drivable...a drive of 135 miles on a mostly two-lane highway which connects numerous islands using 42 bridges. Eventually, you finally arrive in Key West. No more bridges...you're at the end of the line. You cannot go any further south in the United States.

Let's talk about driving. Many people fly to Ft. Lauderdale or Miami and then rent a car. Whichever airport you fly into, get directions to the Florida Turnpike. Go south until it ends in Florida City. It then becomes US 1. You can't get lost; there's only one road. You'll never have to ask directions. You can't make a wrong turn; you just drive!

If you make the drive, take your time and enjoy the trip. It might not seem like many miles but it takes longer than you'd expect. Because there is only one road through the Keys, anything that blocks the road, like an accident, can hold up traffic for hours.

One bumper sticker says "Slow down...this ain't the mainland!" Bad grammar; great thought. Being in a hurry is a contradiction for this visit and you will need an attitude adjustment. Besides that, accidents happen frequently on U.S. 1 because people get impatient, drive too fast or try to pass when they shouldn't. Jimmy Buffett says it best when he sings about "changes in latitude; changes in attitude." Keep that in mind.

One area of highway, called the 18-mile Stretch, is between Florida City and Key Largo. That is the most dangerous area and people are killed in accidents very frequently. **"Slow down...this ain't the mainland!"** We want you to finally

3

arrive in Key West.

Because I have many conversations with people on the phone, planning their trip, they all think they will arrive in Key West much more quickly than is possible. People also call the B&B to book one night. They're going to drive down, stay one night and leave the next day. IT'S NOT WORTH IT!! IT'S TOO LONG A DRIVE!! People just don't realize how long it takes. If you get here for only one night and have to check out and drive hours the next day, IT'S NOT WORTH IT!! Wait until you can at least have one full day with two nights. Trust me on this! It's a longer drive than you think.

OK...I got sidetracked trying to make my point.

I'll save another book for your journey through the Keys. We're trying to get you to Key West. Eventually, you'll get here. One thing you will notice on your drive is that, along the way, are green mile markers beside the road. Directions in the Keys are generally given by referencing the nearest mile marker, commonly written as MM.

Once you get to Key West, you might want your photo taken at **MM0**, at the corner of Whitehead Street and Fleming Street. That signifies the end (or the beginning) of US 1. The other end of it is in Ft. Kent, Maine, at the Canadian Border. In souvenir shops, you will see many green items that are replicas of the MM0 sign.

What are you going to do with that car you rented? Unless you got a great rental rate to keep it, you'll be better off without it. There are many agencies that will rent a car for $30/day at those airports with no drop charge in Key West. Key West is small enough that transportation to locations is easy to find and parking is expensive and at a premium. Towing is big business. Renting bicycles and mopeds is easy. There are plenty of cabs and pedicabs. There is a city transit system and the **Bone Island Shuttle** stops at several of the hotels that are the farthest from downtown.

**Flying?**
**Key West International Airport** is right here on the island. It's

small and very easy to use. The problem is that most of the time, it is very expensive to fly directly here. That's the reason many people drive from another airport. In many cases, if you were flying from Detroit, for example, your roundtrip fare from Detroit to Miami would be equal to the amount of your roundtrip fare between Miami or Ft. Lauderdale and Key West. On many occasions, I have made the direct trip by using Expedia or Travelocity. I might have several stops and an out-of-the-way route but at least I don't have a 4-5 hour drive before my trip starts or when I return.

If you've never driven the Keys, it's an experience and should be done once. After that, it gets old in a hurry! Try to fly. Our airport is small and large planes cannot land here but it's part of the experience. If you don't mind a small plane, try **CapeAir**. It's an incredible sight. This plane is one of my favorites. It illustrates the Conch Republic flag, underwater life, a pirate, treasure, Captain Tony, parrots and more. World renowned artist, Jürek, air-brushed this plane. It so SOOO Key West. For more information, go to http://www.flycapeair.com

**Other Alternatives for getting here**

From both the Ft. Lauderdale and Miami airports, there is the **Keys Shuttle**. It makes round trips between Key West and the two airports several times a day. Call them at 305-289-9997 to find where and when they pickup at each airport.

We have a new Ferry Terminal (that's not Fairy Terminal) that

accommodates the day trips that come from Naples and Ft. Myers Beach. There are also plans for a ferry from Miami. The term "ferry" is somewhat misleading to me. You don't bring a car. It's just a "people" ferry. They do allow you to return on a different day so it makes sense to make it more than a day trip. For more information go to http://www.keywestferry.com or call 800-273-4496.

OK, you're finally here. What do you know about your destination in Paradise?

Don't get in too much of a hurry. Before you can proceed to the next part, I have to test you on what you retained in this section. (Once a teacher, always a teacher!)

## Quiz 1

How many bridges connect the Florida Keys? _____
How long a drive is it? _____
The_____ mile Stretch is very deadly.
Get your picture taken at MM _____ in Key West.
U.S. 1 starts or ends in Key West. The other end is in what state? _____

If you got them all correct, you can go on to the next chapter. (Look them up yourself. It's a take home test.)

# Chapter 2
# What do you know about your destination in Paradise?

**D**o you have any idea about where you're coming…other than what I just told you? If not, don't feel bad; it's a little confusing and misleading.

The day I moved here, I drove 12 hours and I started in Florida (Jacksonville). I always thought that the Keys were just south of Miami or mainland Florida. I learned on that day that, if you have a choice, you try not to be driving toward Key West as the sun is setting. Because it would not occur to me to stop and look at a map, there was plenty to think about as the end of the trip got closer and I was blinded by sun. I couldn't figure out how that could be happening if I was driving south.

When I finally arrived, I called my daughter in Tallahassee (now a Florida State University graduate) and said, "I've arrived but I don't understand how I was driving straight into the sun when I should have been going south. I was going west." As only a smart aleck college student could reply, she said, "Well, duh…why do you think they call it Key WEST?"

She made perfectly good sense (accidentally). When I had a chance, I did look at a map and this chain of islands heads south and then west. In fact, Key West is farther west than the west coast of Florida. While we are geographically linked to the SE coast of Florida, we're really a SW coast of Florida! Who knew?

But, I later found out that Miss FSU daughter wasn't as smart as she thought she was.

Here's the real history of Key West and how it got its name. Pay attention, class! You might be able to win some trivia question some day with this information.

The first people to find this island were Spanish. When they got here, they found bones from Indian burial sites and named the island Cayo Hueso (pronounced KIE-YO HWAY-SO). Say it slowly; maybe you need to try it again. Later as more English speaking people arrived, Cayo Hueso became more Anglicized and became Bone Island. That just didn't sit well as the name for a tourist destination so it then became Key West. Actually, I made that part up but it did become Key West. You can surely see that if you said KIE-YO HWAY-SO often enough that it would get sloppy and become Key West.

All of that to say that FSU daughter was WRONG! Duh...it had nothing to do with being west! That was just a coincidence.

Keep these facts tucked away. You will see things called Cayo Hueso and you will see things with Bone Island...like the Bone Island Shuttle. When you see them, you will immediately perk up because you can give that smug look like you already know it and others don't...and can even pronounce Cayo Hueso. (If you ever win a million dollars because of me, I hope you'll remember who gave you your start!)

Hang in here with me. I'm not too interested in history but I do feel obligated to give you some more facts.

One of those Spaniards ended up owning the island and sold it to John Simonton in 1821. (One of the main streets is Simonton Street. That's why!)

In 1822, it was developed as a navy base and continues, to this day, with three, I repeat, three bases here today although they have been drastically downsized since their peak. Not surprisingly, the Coast Guard is also based here.

There were many pirates in the area. David Porter's Anti-Pirate Squadron helped reduce the number of those scoundrels. (Porter Place is a street here.)

Key West was an important staging area during the Spanish-American war and this lasted through WWI.

Another key player in the development of all of the keys was Henry Flagler. His dream was to build a railroad that would end in Key West. He accomplished that dream. In Key West, he built the Casa Marina Hotel that still stands as the elegant grande dame hotel. He wanted a place for his wealthy friends to stay when they rode the train. Henry Flagler's picture is on the wall on the front of the hotel and the wonderful restaurant is named Flagler's. There is also a railroad museum, Flagler Station, on Caroline Street.

In the early 1900's, bootlegging was a big business as people prepared for Prohibition.

Then came the Depression and the town went bankrupt. In

1935, a horrible hurricane killed many people in the Upper Keys and wiped out the railroad. If you're driving, there is a monument to those killed in the hurricane in Islamorada. At St. Mary's Star of the Sea Catholic Church, on Truman Street, is *Our Lady of Lourdes* grotto built to protect the island from hurricanes. It's worked so far!

WWII came along and again the military brought life back into the island as it was again used as a staging area. When you get here and perhaps go enjoy some time at Smathers Beach, visualize missiles lining that beach during the Bay of Pigs. Strategically, Key West was "the place" if something happened with Cuba!

OK...now you've finished with eight morsels of history and I won't even test you on these because now it's time for the FUN part of the history of Key West and the Florida Keys. Let's go to the **Conch Republic...**

# Chapter 3
# What on earth is
# The Conch Republic?

**Y**ou might not have realized that in your travels you were going to be part of a little known destination called **The Conch Republic.** Like Cayo Hueso and, so that you don't sound like a tourist, you will need to learn how to pronounce CONCH. It's easy; it's KONK. Forget the "ch." KONK, KONK, KONK, KONK, KONK, KONK, KONK! Got it? This is one word you definitely will see over and over.

I know you're saying, "What on earth is a conch?" A conch is a shell with a slug-like animal inside it. You'll see Conch Fritters, Conch Chowder, Conch Salad, etc. But, the term "conch" also refers to those who were born here in Key West. Key West High School teams are Conchs, the dance group is the Conchettes. So learn how to pronounce it. You'll see it referred to often. (Incidentally, the best Conch Fritters are at the Rooftop Café. That's also the place for the best Key Lime Pie in spite of what you'll read at other places! The same lady has worked there 22 years doing nothing but making Key Lime Pie.)

The Conch Shell is the one that you can hold up to your ear and listen to the ocean. It's good luck and you will see many people with a Conch Shell on their porch. BUT…it's BAD LUCK to have it inside. Many people take home Conch Shells as souvenirs but maybe they don't know the true story.

If there was a "Queen Mother" of Key West, it would be Wilhelmina Harvey. Wilhelmina is in her 90's and was born here. She is a CONCH. She's also been the first woman mayor, first woman county commissioner and has many other accolades. She's honored in the Florida Women's Hall of Fame in Tallahassee and was a county commissioner until a few years ago when she was in her late 80's. Her husband was also the Mayor of Key West. Since they were both local political dignitaries, they met all of the famous people who visited. One of those was Queen Elizabeth. Wilhelmina tells the story that she was taken out to the ship to meet the Queen and took her a Conch Shell as a remembrance of Key West. Shortly after the Queen arrived back in England, there was a big fire in the Royal

Palace. Wilhelmina believes it's because she forgot to tell her not to put the Conch Shell inside the palace!

OK...I digressed. Back to the Conch Republic. The Conch Republic was established in 1982 when the Border Patrol decided that a good way to catch illegal aliens, smugglers and other undesirables would be to set up a roadblock north of Key Largo. Traffic jams are bad enough on the road without a road-block so many tourists were fed up with it and decided to go elsewhere. Tourism, which by then, had become a "townsaver" after the military downsized, went south...that is, not to Key West which you know is really west anyway. In other words, the economy suffered greatly.

Conchs are spunky and they are survivors. They got angry and decided to form a separate nation called **The Conch Republic** and secede from the United States. They first seceded and then declared war on the United States. After the secession, the "Civil Rebellion began by breaking a loaf of stale Cuban bread over the head of a man dressed in a U.S. Navy uniform. After one minute of rebellion, they surrendered and demanded 1 Billion dollars in foreign aid and War Relief to rebuild the nation after the long Federal siege!"

There is a Conch Republic flag; there are passports and there is a Secretary General. "We are both Conchs and we are Americans and we are proud to be both. By act of Congress, we hold dual citizenship and will fight for the right to be both! Key West is the nation's capital and the rest of the keys are the 'northern provinces.'"

Every year there is a week long celebration commemorating the big event. Just reading the website gives an idea of the fun that goes with events in the Conch Republic. The slogan, "We

Seceded Where Others Failed" sets the tone. It's all about laughing. They also say:

"As the world's first fith world nation, a sovereign state of mind seeking only to bring more humor, warmth, and respect to a world in sore need of all three, the Conch Republic remains the country who seceded where others failed."

For more information, about The Conch Republic visit the website at http://www.conchrepublic.com

## Quiz 2

How do you pronounce CONCH? _____

# Part II
# Welcome to the Island...
# now what?

# Chapter 4
# Welcome to Paradise!

**K**ey West is an island of unique charm, with lots of art, activities, water sports, fishing, nightlife, music, history and some of the best restaurants to be found anywhere.

There is plenty to see and do while you are in Key West and after you've made that legendary trip down Duval, called the "Duval Crawl," there are butterflies, sightseeing tours, national parks, civil war forts and museums, 6-toed cats at Hemingway's House, ghost tours, dolphin watch and millions of dollars in gold treasure.

Go sightseeing and discover the natural beauty and images of the past that make Key West truly unique. Whether you are looking for a day on the water, a day on the land, a leisurely walking tour around the island, bike riding, a fabulous meal or just a taxi…it's all here. Your concierge can help you or I can if you don't have one. All of the activities I recommend have been given my "Stamp of Approval," so I know you will have the best time on your Key West vacation.

### IMAGINE...

People...Culture...History: An island of charm, eccentricity and diversity. Unique for its art and architecture. Alive with possibilities as boundless as the turquoise sea. Wake up to the rhythm of the tropics (or the sound of roosters) and paradise to explore and savor.

*Johnson, Pat, "Courtyard by Marriott Concierge Brochure"*

# Chapter 5
# First time in Key West?

**H**ere's your primer!

Key West is probably one of the best known small towns any-where! It is small enough, it is rumored, to fit into NYC's Central Park. Key West has managed, through its' rich history, remote location and natural beauty to earn a notation in nearly every national and international map.

Our island is only 2 miles x 4 miles. There is no uptown or downtown in Key West. (There is Old Town and New Town though.) Tolerance is the rule and differences are to be cele-brated and accepted. Our City Commission and our County Commission both have officially adopted the motto conceived by J.T. Thompson:

# ONE HUMAN FAMILY

Even daily life in Key West includes a certain offbeat sense of celebration. Each day's setting sun is celebrated and applauded at Mallory Square...and a must for your first visit here.

**Dress Code:** Key West Casual is the rule. Most restaurants, even the most upscale, will serve you if you're wearing a shirt, shoes and shorts.

Dressed up people in the Keys are referred to as Bride, Groom or Defendant!

What does a Conch say when he's dressed up in a suit and tie? "Not guilty, your honor!"

**Parking:** A premium in Key West; you'll pay for every inch of real estate you park on. Meters run from 6 am until midnight and cost about $1.00/hour. Have plenty of quarters if you're fortunate enough to find a place. You will get a ticket and they're BIG revenue here.

*\*Above copy is mostly "lifted" right from the Courtyard by Marriott Concierge Brochure by Pat Johnson, but I added to it.*

**Watch Out!** Many T-shirts stores are the bane of our existence. We try to regulate and fine them but they pay the fine and con-tinue to try to bilk tourists. Check Albertson's, Walgreen's or K-Mart for a great selection and almost all are embroidered—for about $10. Of course, you need a car but they're all on N. Roosevelt Blvd....which is a different name for Truman Ave.

The other big problem is the bums who sit on the sidewalk. (Homeless is one thing; bum is another!) Please don't pay attention to them and PLEASE don't reward them by giving them money! Just ignore them. Lots of legal issues prevent the city from being able to take action. We're not ignoring the problem...in spite of how it may appear!

**Streets to know:** The main street leading into town is Truman Avenue. Before it becomes Truman Ave., it is called N. Roosevelt Blvd. The reality is that it is US 1. Don't get confused if you're driving. Those are all different names for the same street.

Duval Street is the main street. If you are not directionally challenged, as I am, you will realize that it runs north and south. Duval Street is the 'longest street in the world' as it runs from the Gulf of Mexico to the Atlantic Ocean. Clever, isn't it, but it really is only a little over a mile from "sea to shining sea!" **Duval Street is the main street you need to know.**

Running parallel to Duval Street is Simonton Street. (That name should be familiar to you. Who was Mr. Simonton?) On the other side of Duval Street , running parallel to it, is Whitehead Street. Those are the three main north and south streets in the area known as Old Town.

As you come into town, probably on Truman, the intersection of Truman and Duval is a good reference point. If you turn RIGHT on Duval and continue to the end, you will pass the busiest part of town. The closer you get to that end, the busier (and louder) it gets.

Turning left on Duval at Truman, will take you a shorter distance to the end but it is the quieter end. Because you are going South then, that's where you will find the Southernmost Point, the Southernmost House, the Southernmost Resort, etc. While there are many art galleries all over the island, many of them are at that end of Duval Street.

Besides Truman Avenue, other streets that intersect with Duval Street are Eaton, Caroline, Greene, Fleming (one way out), Southard (one way in), South, United and other smaller ones in between.

When I moved here, I used to get lost often. But, the best thing is that you can't drive endlessly. Sooner or later you're going to run into water. If you begin to know the main streets going each direction, when you accidentally run into one, it will help you know what you're close to.

**Transportation:** As I mentioned earlier, it's best to avoid using your car unless you have a handicapped tag. Parking is expensive and hard to find. Consider renting bicycles or mopeds but BE CAREFUL. People are so careless on vacation and "hot dog." Tourists are KILLED every year on mopeds. Get them but drive them carefully. Your hotel might have an arrangement with a business which rents scooter or bikes. If not, my favorite place for bikes and mopeds is **Moped Hospital** on the corner of Truman and Simonton.

Another alternative is the electric cars. They are expensive but the ones I love to see are those that are rented by **Monarch Custom Cars** at 1020 Duval Street. They're not just the typical electric cars you see cruising around. These are all special designs, like a 50's convertible or a truck. They're cute with several choices for your special car.

Handicapped? Long time overdue is a business to accommodate those needing assistance getting around. **Keys Krawlers** is located at 720 Caroline Street and their phone number is 305-797-6914. They have wheelchairs and motorized scooters for handicapped people. Just remember...sidewalks and streets are narrow and bumpy. While efforts are always being made to make things as handicapped accessible as possible, things are improving but there's a long way to go!

# Chapter 6
# Let's get started!

**W**hether you're here for one night or one week, there are two things you need to make a priority. You need to take a ride on the Old Town Trolley and you need to hope for good weather so you can be part of the Sunset Celebration.

**Old Town Trolley:** As soon as you can after you arrive, plan to take the Trolley. It takes 11/2 hours, although you can get on and off until you reach your starting point. There is always one 30 minutes behind you to get back on. The Conch Tour Train and the Trolley are both owned by Historic Tours of America, cost the same amount of money BUT the Trolley goes around the entire island; the Train only goes around Old Town. And, you can get on and off the Trolley. I recommend the Trolley. Tickets are $22 but it is the best thing you can do to become oriented to the island. Do it early in your trip. Then, when people give you directions you have an idea about the location. You'll also see places on the tour that you might want to go back to. All in all, it's the best way to learn about much of the history of the island, the trees and flowers, which famous people have lived in which houses and much more interesting history than I've given you. I've been on it many times with my own guests and still, always learn something else that I didn't know or had forgotten. It's a definite "must do" for my own guests and for guests at the B&B. There are several locations around town where you can board the trolley and the train. The most central is at the corner of Truman and Duval but ask at your hotel where the closest location is for you.

**Sunset at Mallory Square:** We're famous for our Sunset Celebration. (We know…that same sun sets all over the world but we celebrate just about anything and sunset is one of those celebrations.) We even have a Sunset Celebration when there is no sunset…unless it's really raining!

The most famous place to celebrate is at **Mallory Square**. That's at the north, or busy, end of Duval. Go to the stoplight at the end of Duval (the corner of Duval and Front Streets) and continue on Duval. You will be walking between the **Pier House Hotel** on the right and the **Ocean Key House** on the left. Turn left on the little street (Wall Street) by the Ocean Key House and walk about a half block. You will see the parking lot and people heading toward Mallory Square. Just follow them and hope there are no cruise ships blocking your view; 12 nights a year they are allowed to stay and that's a bummer! Mallory Square consists of street performers and vendors. Your hotel staff or the daily newspaper will tell you what time sunset is.

I suggest going to Mallory Square early, walk around and say "been there, done that" and then…retrace your steps back down the little street to the extension of Duval Street. Again, you're right between the Ocean Key House and the Pier House. Turn left and walk out to the very end of the pier. **The Billiefish Bar**, part of the Ocean Key House, is my favorite place to find a table and sit, have a Margarita, listen to the live music and watch a beautiful sunset. It simply doesn't get any better that!

If there are no seats available there, see if you have any better luck at **Havana Docks**. It's on an upper level and part of the Pier House. You'll be able to turn around and see it from Billiefish so it will be easy to figure out how to get there.

**Other Sunset Suggestions: The Hilton Pier** has become another venue for celebrating sunset. From the stop light at the end of Duval Street, turn left on Front Street and go to the end. The Hilton Hotel is there. Walk down beside the hotel and follow the crowd.

If you're here more than one night, make it a point to observe sunset from **The Top** of the **LaConcha Hotel** at the corner of Duval and Fleming. The LaConcha is the "highrise" in town! (And, so that you can avoid sounding like a tourist, this is pronounced just like it's spelled. Just when you thought you understood Conch, adding an "a" at the end doesn't make this hotel the LaKonka.) The LaConcha is a Crowne Plaza Hotel these days. There is a bar at the top. The easiest way to get there is to go through **Starbucks** from Duval and out their back door. Right there is an elevator. Take it to The Top.

If you can't go for sunset, then definitely just go during the day to view Key West from "on high." It's beautiful. There's a camera up there and the NBC station in Miami shows shots from there nearly every morning during the *Today Show*.

**Turtle Kraals** restaurant on the harbor has a tower bar.

There are surprisingly few restaurants with good sunset views. Those that do are all upscale restaurants. Those with the best view are **Hot Tin Roof** at the **Ocean Key House, One Duval** at the Pier House and **Latitudes** at **Sunset Key** (Hilton). Nowhere else compares to their locations.

Finally, there are many choices for sunset on the water. A sunset cruise is lots of fun. My favorite is the **Western Union**. The ship has a history and is a beautiful work of art. They serve complimentary wine, beer, soft drinks and champagne. During the summer they often serve Key Lime Sherbet and in the winter, they often serve Conch Chowder as well. A musician is on board who sings sea shanties and they invite anyone who wants to participate to help raise the sails.

The Western Union also has a Stargazer Cruise that goes out after the Sunset Cruise. If you're interested in stars and planets, this is the cruise for you on a clear night. They provide the binoculars.

There are other choices. You're better off asking than walking up to any kiosk on the street. Ask your hotel concierge or contact the Keys to Paradise virtual concierge service at http://www.keystoparadise.info. I want you to have a great visit and that means making good choices for your activities.

## Quiz 3

What is the high rise in town? _____
Where is our most famous Sunset Celebration? _____

# Chapter 7
# My personal very special suggestions

In later chapters, I'm going to go more in detail but some things might get lost in all the minutiae, I mean information, that you're going to get. There are just some things that I want to present in a special section. Why...because they're special to me and you might not find some of them on your own.

I'm pretty sure you won't want to miss the **Butterfly and Nature Conservatory**. This is one of the newest businesses in town and what a wonderful response it has gotten! It's located at the South end of Duval Street. You can't miss it...a two story yellow building with a huge atrium structure in the back. It is an attraction that we are all proud of. The conservatory is terrific with thousands of butterflies and birds. Cost is $10 for adults. Most concierges have cards that give you 10% off. Conservatory is terrific; gift shop is awesome! The special wall hangings, using butterflies, are a must have gift for yourself. Look for the pictures that are made using broken butterfly wings; they're easy to miss. If you don't see them, ask one of the attendants to show you. Also, in the jewelry section, notice the jewelry which uses broken butterfly wings. None are the same. They're beautiful. I always get comments on my necklace. For more info and to order online, go to http://www.keywestbutterfly.com

While you're at that end of Duval, go take your photo at the **Southernmost Point**. Turn right at the next corner (Duval and South). You'll see it! Truthfully, it's not the real Southernmost Point. I'm sorry to be the one to break it to you. A few years ago there was talk of moving it but certain factions in the community wanted it to stay so it stayed! It has recently been renovated. So, get your picture taken there and no one at home will ever know that you weren't really at the southernmost point in the United States. It will be our little secret!

At that same corner (1400 Duval Street) is the **Southernmost House**. It has recently been opened. It is open to the public from 8 am to 8 pm, For $8 you have all day access to their pool and bar. There is a very interesting short tour of the house/museum. It's one of the loveliest sites for a wedding.

While you're in the area, visit this house. It truly is a beautiful place with an impressive history. For more info before you get here, go to http://www.TheMansionatKeyWest.com

For walking and biking tours, a wonderful resource is **Sharon Wells' Walking and Biking Guide to Historic Key West** (free). The **Cemetery Tour** is one of the most popular. You will see the tombstone that says *"I told you I was sick"* and the wife who put on her husband's grave, *"At least I know where you're sleeping tonight."*

Besides the Cemetery Tour, there are 13 other tours in the guide that you can take on your own either by walking or bicycles.

Your concierge should have copies or they're at many distribution points around the city. Go to http://www.seekeywest.com for more information. Sharon also is an artist and has a small gallery at 534 Fleming Street, next to Fausto's Market. Each time she updates her guide, she has one of her paintings on the front. They can be purchased at her website and are lovely when they're matted and framed.

If you have an extra full day, plan on a trip to **Fort Jefferson at the Dry Tortugas National Park**. It is an all day trip if you go by boat or a 4-hour trip by plane. Fort Jefferson was built in the mid-1800's and they used over 16 million bricks. It took over 30 years and was never finished and never used as a fort. It was, however, used as a military prison during the Civil War, mostly for deserters. But the most famous prisoners were the 4 men convicted of complicity in President Abraham Lincoln's assassination in 1865. The most famous of them was Dr. Samuel Mudd. His family continues to this day to clear his name. The self-directed tour takes about 45 minutes. You can snorkel while you're there or just find a hammock and read. There is a campground. Reservations are required and there is a $5 charge for park admission. Definitely a must if you have the time.

Noteworthy shops include **Peppers of Key West** (take your own beer and sit and sample...if you're in to HOT!) Located at 602 Greene Street, it might be easy to find if the "Pepper Car" happens to be parked in front. That's a photo op as well.

**Kermit's Key West Key Lime Shoppe** at the corner of Elizabeth and Greene, just a half a block from Peppers. Be sure to get their Key Lime Pie on a Stick and take home a little container of Key Lime Pepper. His Key Lime Thimble Cookies pack or send easily. **Don't be fooled by imitations.** There are lots of places with similar names.

**Fast Buck Freddie's** looks like a "dime store" on Duval Street. Trust me...it's not! However, there's also **Half Buck Freddie's** on Caroline Street, close to B.O.'s.

**Pelican Poop** at 314 Simonton Street has great Caribbean merchandise. Take the little tour at Pelican Poop. It's an unusual building with an historic background that involves Ernest Hemingway. And, next to Pelican Poop is the **T-Shirt Factory**. One of the "good," ethical t-shirt stores.

**Nancy's Secret Garden** is off the 500 block of Simonton Street, down a little alley called Free School Lane. If you like tropical gardens, you'll love this spot.

**Monty's Conch Harbor Restaurant** at 951 Caroline Street is new with a huge, beautiful pool and waterfall. The pool is open to the public! FREE! If you're staying somewhere without a pool, you've got a beautiful one now. FREE! It's close to the Ferry Terminal, Turtle Kraals and Half Shell Raw Bar. And, the pool is FREE!

## QUIZ 4

What restaurant has a FREE pool? _____

If you got the answer correct, "Let's Eat"

# Chapter 8
# Finally, let's eat!

**K**ey West is an island of unique charm, with lots of art, activities, water sports, fishing, nightlife, music, history and some of the best restaurants to be found anywhere.

For such a small town, it is amazing that there are over 300 restaurants. Even more amazing is the fact that most of them are excellent or very good.

Whatever you're looking for, you can probably find it. But, recommending restaurants is such a personal opinion. All I can do is suggest places that I hear consistently good reports about. There are never any guarantees but my suggestions will probably serve you better than walking down the street and taking your chances!

The number of meals you have in Key West are limited and I want you to have the best experiences with all of them. I don't want you to waste a meal opportunity somewhere that I could have steered you away from.

If you were to ask me, I would ask you:
- What atmosphere do you want...on the water, outside, or you don't care?
- What kind of food?
- What are you expecting to spend?

When I know the answers to those questions, I'll do my best to direct you to the place that seems to fit your criteria.

Remember...just ask! Your concierge will be happy to make reservations for you or give you suggestions...and so will I. At some places, I know the special tables to ask for.

## QUIZ 5

How many restaurants are there on this small island? \_\_\_\_\_

# Special consideration restaurants

**Blue Heaven** at 729 Thomas Street (corner of Thomas and Petronia) in Bahama Village. If you went by there and no one told you, you probably would stay away **but do not leave Key West** without going to Blue Heaven. I like it best for breakfast. Great food, reasonable price and an atmosphere like no other. It is open for lunch and dinner as well. I've never had guests visit me that were allowed to leave if we didn't go to Blue Heaven for breakfast. Breakfast and lunch $$; dinner is $$$.

**Pepe's** at 806 Caroline is also excellent for all three meals but breakfast is a favorite. My 2nd favorite for breakfast. My sister and family, from Michigan, stayed an extra day so that her husband could go back to Pepe's for breakfast. And, we recently had to replace his favorite Pepe's shirt. Prices similar to Blue Heaven.

**B.O.'s Fish Wagon** is on the corner of Caroline and William Street. Another place that you might avoid when you see it but this "shack" has been featured in National Geographic. DON'T go there and order a hamburger. It's a fish place! Excellent fish sandwiches. Go in and act like you know what you're doing by ordering a "special." That will get you a fish sandwich and fries. You can also act extremely knowledgeable and ask for half and half to drink. That's half ice tea and half lemonade. B.O. (Buddy Owens) catches the fish daily. When my cousin, George, comes from Chicago, he goes there EVERY SINGLE DAY. Great for lunch! $$

**Meteor Smokehouse** at 404 Southard Street. If you like barbecue, this is the place but, if you like HOT, you must try an order of Minnie Lee's Beans. They'll clear your sinuses but they're delicious. They're not baked beans; they're green beans. $$

Attached to the Meteor is the Green Parrot Bar...one of the best known watering holes.

**Big John's Pizza** has recently opened a location in Old Town. They're located at 610 Greene Street but they also deliver. Their "Stuffed John" is incredible but there are lots of other choices. $

**Damn Good Food to Go** is located on the Historic Waterfront, between A&B Lobster House and Commodore

Steak House. They deliver in Old Town from 6am to midnight.
$

**Hog's Breath Saloon** is at the corner of Duval and Front Street.
I normally stay away from recommending "corporate" but they
do have good fish sandwiches and sinful chili cheese fries…my
daughter's favorite! $$

Blue Heaven restaurant

# Doesn't fall in other categories!

**The Blond Giraffe** has a location at 629 Duval Street and one at 1209 Truman. They have good Key Lime Pie but I, personally, don't think it's the best. What I do love there is their maté drink. The owners are from Brazil and maté is from there. It is an unusual coffee type drink (but not really). I can't really describe it and maybe it's an acquired taste but I enjoy it. You can get Key Lime Pie there if you want. They've won the People's Choice Award for it. It's just not my personal favorite. It's a nice shop with lots of Key Lime products.

**Flamingo Crossing** is at 1107 Duval Street. If you like ice cream, make it a stop. It's all homemade daily and includes many tropical flavors.

**Grand Vin** is next door (same owners). They have wine tastings every afternoon.

**Key West Winery** at 107 Simonton Street. Stop by to taste unusual but delicious wines like Key Lime, Mango, etc.

**Dennis Pharmacy** at the corner of Simonton and United. It has an old time counter and some tables. It is a Key West experience. Jimmy Buffett made "Cheeseburger in Paradise" something to want to experience and you can get it at his Margaritaville restaurant. But, his idea began at the Dennis Pharmacy...and it's a lot cheaper!

**Croissants de France** is at 816 Duval Street. They have always been open for breakfast and lunch with wonderful fresh baked pastries but they have recently opened for dinner as well.

**Coffee and Tea House of Key West**, located at 1218 Duval Street, is a little house. Get what you want and sit out on the porch and watch the other tourists go by. This is not a coffee shop like you find in every airport and city. It has its' own uniqueness.

**Waterfront Market** at the Historic Seaport, behind B.O.'s Fishwagon, at the corner of Caroline and William Street. An out of the ordinary grocery store with an internet café upstairs.

# Chapter 9
# What about the other
# 300+ restaurants?

**OK**...you've been very patient so here we are with...the rest of the (restaurant) story! I'm certainly not going to mention 300 but I am going to tell you the ones I think are top choices out of that big group. I know I'll leave someone's favorite out but this is my honest list of places I would recommend. (Remember no one knows I'm writing this so I'm not being paid for including any restaurant or shop because I want this to be totally my recommendations. Now, I'm not beholden to anyone!) Of course, I have my favorites where I usually take my own guests but, odds are, answering the questions I gave you earlier will help match you up to something good. Do you remember those questions? Here they are again but this is the last time I'm telling you:

• What atmosphere do you want...on the water, outside, or you don't care?
• What kind of food?
• What are you expecting to spend?

**Here are my picks for Fabulous Upscale Dining Experiences:**
I'll do these alphabetically so I don't offend anyone.

**A&B Lobster House**, at the end of Front Street on the waterfront. On the second floor, it has a very nice harbor view but not good for sunset. Inside and outside dining. Elegant. Of course, seafood is the specialty but you can't go wrong with anything you order. $$$$

**Alice's on Duval**, across from La te da. New location (really back to her old location). Alice is an award-winning chef. They serve breakfast, lunch, dinner and Sunday brunch. $$$

**Antonia's**, 615 Duval Street. Great Italian food. During the summer, they have a Hurricane Special (better known as Early Bird in other locales). It's a great deal and always excellent. $$$

**Bagatelle Restaurant** at 115 Duval Street. Lovely house, garden and food. $$$

**Bistro 245** on the pier at the Hilton. Looks at Sunset Key. Both casual and elegant dining; inside and outside seating. Range of prices. On Friday and Saturday evenings, enjoy a combination elegant dinner and the music of Spanish guitarist, Matthew Jampol.

**Café Marquesa**, on the corner of Fleming and Southard. Inside, no waterfront but elegant. $$$$

**Café Med**, on the corner of Fleming and Grinnell. Mostly inside, wonderful food. $$$

**Café Sole** at 1029 Southard Street. Wonderful dinner and Sunday brunch. Not on the water but most tables are outside. $$$

**Commodore**, at the end of Front Street, next to A&B on the waterfront. Terrific steaks and seafood, great location overlooking A&B Marina. $$$$

**Flagler's** at the Casa Marina Hotel. The Casa Marina is the grande dame hotel of Key West...old and elegant. Built by Henry Flagler when he brought the railroad to Key West, the hotel has survived; the railroad didn't. Flagler's is elegant but all year they have their Early Evening Special from 6-8. Music every night as well. $$$$

**Hot Tin Roof** in the Ocean Key House at the end of Duval Street. An upscale place to be at sunset (or anytime). Beautiful location and very interesting menu which they call Conch Fusion. $$$$

**Kelly's**, formerly owned by actress Kelly McGillis on Whitehead and Caroline. Beautiful garden, good food. $$$

**Key West Seafood and Beer Garden** at 519 Duval Street. Fabulous food in a lovely outdoor garden with foliage and ponds. $$$

**Latitudes** on Sunset Key, across from the Hilton Hotel. Great food, great location. You must have reservations as you'll take the boat from Hilton Marina. $$$$

**La Trattoria** on the corner of Duval Street and Applerouth Lane. Elegant Italian. **Virgilio's** bar, in the back, is a favorite for live music. $$$$

**Louie's Backyard** at the corner of Vernon and Wadell. Even if you don't go there for a meal, go for a drink at the **Afterdeck**, overlooking the ocean. $$$$

**Mangia Mangia Pasta Café** at 903 Southard Street. Indoor and outdoor patio; no view. $$$

**Mangoe's** at 700 Duval Street. Mostly outside, great food. $$$

**Martha's** on S. Roosevelt Blvd., close to the airport. Nice view, overlooking the ocean, and nice ambience. $$$$

**Martin's** on Appelrouth Lane. German food; excellent Sunday brunch. $$$

**Michael's** at 532 Margaret Street. Always excellent. Go in late afternoon to have fondue at the bar! $$$

**Nicola's** at the Hyatt Hotel on Front Street. Sometimes good for sunset; great atmosphere and food. $$$

**One Duval** at Pier House Hotel. Beautiful, elegant dining on the water. Piano music in the bar. $$$$

**Pisces**, 1001 Simonton Street. Great food, posh place. $$$$

**Rooftop Café** on Front Street, upstairs. Lovely patio dining or inside. Early menu in the summer. Live music every night. **The best conch fritters on the island**, in my opinion, and **the best Key Lime Pie**. $$$

**Seven Fish** at 632 Olivia. This eclectic place seats 20 and serves 7 fish selections every night...all great! $$$

**Salute** at Higgs Beach on Atlantic Blvd. Overlooks the beach. Great for lunch and dinner. $$$

**Shula's** at The Reach Hotel at the end of Simonton Street. Corporate but geared to Key West...excellent seafood and steaks. Side dishes serve more than one. Wonderful location. Early special menu in the summer. $$$$

**Square One** in Duval Square. Last but not least...probably my favorite BUT it's inside, no view. A locals favorite, especially for special occasions. Breakfast, lunch, dinner and Sunday Brunch. Wonderful menu/bar. Piano nightly. $$$

### Not Quite so Elegant but recommended!

**Abbondanza** at 1208 Simonton Street. Excellent pasta dishes. $$

**Banana Café** at 1211 Duval Street. Predominantly French; delicious crepes. $$

**Camille's** at 1202 Simonton Street. Inside, varied menu. Breakfast, lunch, dinner. $$

**Caroline's** at 310 Duval. Great for lunch or lighter dinner. $$

**Duval Beach Club** at the very end of Duval Street. They'll serve you on the beach. $

**El Meson de Pepe's** at Mallory Square. Outside. Great Cuban food for lunch or dinner. $$

**El Siboney** at 900 Catherine Street. A local authentic Cuban restaurant. The real thing; nothing fancy. Closed Sunday; no credit cards. $$

**Finnegan's Wake** at Caroline and Grinnell. Good Irish food, bar, music. $$

**Fogarty's** and **Flying Monkey Bar** on the corner of Duval and Caroline. Great place for lunch, casual dinner. The place for an outside sports bar. Great food, huge portions, reasonable prices. $$

**Garden Café** at 917 Duval Street. Small little garden area serving breakfast, lunch and dinner. $$

**Grand Café** at 314 Duval Street. Outside, great lunch and dinner. Besides an interesting menu with some terrific dishes, they also have pizza. $$

**Jamaican Me Hungry** upstairs at 300 Front Street. Terrific, authentic Jamaican cuisine. Say hi to Warren and Abby. They've had the business for many years but previously it was at a motel by the airport where the Beatles once stayed. That motel is gone and the space is now a Hyatt time-share. $$

**New York Pizza Café** in Duval Square. Much more than pizza; huge sandwiches. $$

**Old Town Mexican Café** at 609 Duval Street. If you must have Mexican in Key West, here's the place. $$

**Origami** in Duval Square. Great sushi. $$

**Sands Beach Club** at the end of Simonton Street. Great sandwiches and salad bar at lunch. Dinner menu varies. They will even serve you on the beach. $$

**The Café** at 509 Southard Street. Vegetarian with other choices. $

**Turtle Kraals** on the waterfront. Parking lot on Caroline Street if you drive. Ideal for your first night in town. Key West atmosphere on the harbor. A favorite because it's not unusual to have someone's dog or cat with them. Looks like a sports bar without the TV's. Lots of seafood and other great food with a Caribbean flair. I probably send more people here than any other restaurant. $$

### Out of Old Town or Off the Island

If you have a car, you can experience some other places that locals enjoy.

**Chico's Cantina** on Stock Island is another Mexican restaurant. Good food, outdoor patio dining. On US 1 across from the golf course. $$

**Courtyard Café** at the Courtyard by Marriott, next to IHOP. Allan and Linda have been serving food at various locations for many years. Locals were thrilled when they began their little café at the hotel a few years ago. Breakfast and lunch only. Lovely setting, great food and friendly staff. A favorite for all of us here. A lot of business is conducted at the Courtyard Café over lunch! $

**Hickory House** on Stock Island. Locals favorite and great Jazz Sunday brunch. $$

**Hurricane Joe's** also on U.S. 1 on Stock Island. Relatively new. $$

**Rusty Anchor** at 5510 3rd Ave. on Stock Island. (That address won't be helpful at all. I always get lost going there.) Ask someone how to get there. I think it's easy if the right person tells you. But, it is THE BEST fresh seafood around. Nothing fancy here. It's very very local but if you want the place where locals go for seafood that isn't touristy, this is the place. $$

Now, if you can't find great food from this list, I give up on you! Don't even complain to me; I'll have no sympathy and I'll be hurt! I'm doing the best I can for you!

# Chapter 10
# What else is there to do?

**D**id I hear you say, "What else is there to do?" I already gave you starter suggestions in Chapter 7 but now let's go into more detail. Just remember, things constantly change and businesses come and go. There are so many choices in each category but I'm only going to give you ones that I've had good reports on and with people who are easy to work with. These are in no particular order.

We are an island, surrounded by water. It stands to reason that our most popular activities, off Duval Street, are water activities. Let's start with an easy one.

### Beaches and Other Things Close to the Beaches

Our beaches might not be what you expect a Florida beach to be. In their natural state, they're not great because we're surrounded by the wonderful coral reef. Therefore, we have no waves and walking in the water is rough...you're walking on coral shell. **Smathers Beach** and **Higgs Beach** are small but pretty. The sand is brought in from the Bahamas. They'll serve your sunning needs. The **Ft. Zachary Taylor State Park** beach is beautiful, very natural, uncommercialized and you can ONLY snorkel there. The other two beaches are too shallow.

Both Smathers Beach and Higgs Beach are on the same side of the island (south).

**Smathers Beach** is the longest and runs alongside S. Roosevelt Blvd. from Bertha Street to the end of the island. It goes past the airport. It is pretty and will serve your needs for a beach to lie in the sun. There are food vendors and water sports vendors. Whether you're walking, biking or driving on the street or sidewalk beside the beach, take notice of the decorative tiles on a portion of the wall. This is a new project, one of several, sponsored by the **Art In Public Places** Board. This particular project is by **Debra Yates**, one of the island's most recognized artists and she's a Conch! We all wish the entire wall could be done.

On S. Roosevelt Blvd., by the airport, is the **East Martello Museum**. This fort was built during the Civil War but was never used as a fort. Currently the Key West Art and Historical Society operates a museum filled mostly with local historical art and memorabilia. Robert, the spooky doll from the Ghost Tours is in a case there and is very, well…spooky!

**Higgs Beach** is between White Street and Reynolds on Atlantic Blvd. It's much smaller but is a favorite. Along that portion of Atlantic Blvd., there are the ruins of the **West Martello Tower**. The **Key West Garden Club** is located in there now. The beautiful setting has a seaside view and lots of orchids and other plants.

Notice the historic marker along Atlantic Blvd. by the fort denoting the **African Burial Ground**. In 2000, it was discovered that there were 294 Africans buried there. The Navy tried to rescue African slaves from the slave ships and successfully rescued over 1400. Many of them were brought to Key West but in 1860, 294 died.

Along the same stretch of Higgs Beach is the restaurant, **Salute**. I mentioned it earlier but while you're there, it's a nice place for lunch or dinner. It's a favorite of mine for lunch.

Used with permission of Seattle Post-Intelligencer, David Horsey cartoon, published July 18, 2004.

At the very end of Atlantic Blvd. and Higgs Beach, as Atlantic turns onto Reynolds Street at the Casa Marina Hotel is **Dick**

**Dock**. Nice place to go for a walk; don't ask where it got its name!

In the same area, at the end of White Street, is the **White Street Pier**. It is a wonderful place to walk or fish and a favorite for walking dogs…so watch your step. All the way out on the end, the Sunrise Rotary has painted a giant compass with points to various locations…like Cuba. Right at the corner of White Street and Atlantic Blvd., at the beginning of the pier, is the **AIDS Memorial**. AIDS is a disease we're all very aware of here. Most of us have friends who are affected or have died from AIDS. The AIDS Memorial is a beautiful monument to the memory of people who have made wonderful contributions to this community.

Blocking the access to the pier to drivers, is another decorative project commissioned by the **Art in Public Places** Board. The tiled stanchions and planters are by **Wally McGregor**. (Wally is a she.)

In a totally different location and end of town, is **Ft. Zachary Taylor State Park**. Find Southard Street, which is one way. It runs perpendicular to Duval Street. Go as far as you can go on Southard Street and you will then enter a gated community, called Truman Annex. Go past the guard house, straight ahead and you will see signs to the park. There is a small entrance charge. Drive on back in there and you will find a fort, oddly enough named Ft. Zachary Taylor, and a beach that is the favorite of locals.

The fort was built to be able to observe both the Atlantic Ocean and the Gulf of Mexico and was used during the Civil War, the Spanish American War, WWI and WWII.

The beach is 1000 feet long but there is no soft sand brought in there like the other two beaches. It's a beautiful place for sunset and many sunset weddings take place there. As I mentioned before, it's the only beach where it's deep enough to snorkel. They also have Segway Tours there. Segway's are not allowed to be ridden in Old Town Key West, much to my disappointment.

There are few hotels with their own beaches. The Casa

Marina, The Reach and some of the properties of the Southernmost Resorts have nice beaches. If you stay at the Hilton, you have access to the beach at Sunset Key. The Ocean Key House, Pier House and Hyatt all have small beach areas. Grand Key Resort rents a portion of Smathers beach for guests and provides their own bus transportation there. And, the Sheraton Suites is across the street from the beach but not right on it.

Finally, we never forget our pets. There is **Dog Beach** right next to Louie's Backyard Restaurant at the corner of Vernon and Waddell. It's a tiny little piece of space where people take their dogs to swim. Even if you don't have a dog, stop by and watch.

That's the story of beaches and other surrounding sites at the beaches. One final note...check beach advisories. They are often polluted...a problem of most South Florida beaches. And, don't forget the sunscreen!

*Photo credit: Peter Arnow*

AIDS Memorial

# Chapter 11
## (not bankruptcy yet)
## Fishing

**M**any people come to the Keys to fish and there are many different ways to do it. It helps to know what kind of fishing you want to do but some of that is determined by the season. There are plenty of knowledgeable captains who will be happy to help you if you simply don't know. For many people, it's part of the experience and perhaps something that you know nothing about. Don't worry; they're used to it. In fact, they're probably more used to people who don't know much because many people who are knowledgeable have their own boats or rent or charter their own trip.

There are so many ways to do your fishing and so many boats that you won't have a problem. There are marinas on Stock Island. If you're driving into town, when you get into Key West, the first one you will see is **Garrison Bight Marina** at the corner of Roosevelt Blvd. and Palm Ave. If you turn right at that stop light, there are marinas on both sides. Garrison Bight Marina is on the right; **Charterboat Row** is on the left.

Incidentally, the restaurant on the left, just past Charterboat Row, is called **Harbor Lights**. The downstairs part is a bar. The James Bond movie, *Licence to Kill*, had one scene where a boat crashed into THAT bar. ("License" isn't misspelled; that's what it is…the British spelling.)

Other marinas are in Old Town at the Hilton and all around the wharf. They have different names but they are all basically in the same location.

### Boat Rental
I've had people ask where they can rent a boat. Oddly enough, I've only found one place, the **Key West Boat Company**. Call 305-294-2628 to discuss what they have available.

### Inexpensive Fishing on a Large Boat
If you really don't know what you're doing and just want to go out so you can say you went fishing and you don't want to spend much money, a boat like **Capt. John's Greyhound V** will suit your needs. This is a 5-hour trip that provides everything

you will need. Cost is $30 for adults and $20 for children. It's a great way to take a family without spending as much money as other choices because there are a lot of people on the boat. It's definitely the low budget way to go but serves the purpose for many.

## Split Charter

What many people want to do is split the cost of a charter boat with others, often strangers. These boats are small, usually accommodating 6-8 people. Most of them offer half day and full day charters. You rent a chair and everything is provided. Or, the boat can be chartered so that it doesn't include strangers. Average half day costs to rent a chair are about $125-150.

Charters that I have used for guests repeatedly, with great feedback, include the following:

**Fishbuster** at 296-9969
**Fish Check** at 295-0484
**Rampage** at 296-7996
**Relentless** at 304-3043

## Deep Sea Fishing and Light Tackle

Deep Sea Fishing is the "granddaddy" of fishing, romanticized by Ernest Hemingway and the experience that many people MUST have on their Keys vacation. Most people who enjoy fishing, or those who've never tried, have visions of that mounted sailfish on the wall in their home or office. Or, they just want the opportunity to try so they can tell about "the one that got away!" Going deep sea fishing usually means fishing for sailfish, marlin, tuna, dolphin, snapper, grouper or tarpon. But, the time of year determines what's running. Half day trips range from $350-550. Full day trips are generally between $550-$800.

There are many and many I don't know but I do know these:
**Sailfish** at 295-3369
**Heavy Hitter Charters** at 745-6665
**Amoross Charters** at 296-7674

**Triple Time/Jolly Roger** at 296-8210
**Blue Water Charters** at 304-8888

### Flats and Backcountry

When you go out on one of these boats, you generally will go to more remote spots. In many cases, you can go snorkeling while you're out there. The small boats usually accommodate 4 and they provide everything. It's very personal. Cost is similar to deep sea fishing above. My favorites are:

**Bone Island Charters** at 293-0597
**Fishing the Flats of Key West** at 745-2114
**Phil Thompson** at 304-0830

# Chapter 12
# Other "On the Water/
# In the Water" Activities

Besides fishing, there are many other ways to spend time, either in or on the water. There are so many choices. Basically, it just depends on the kind of experience you want.

### Diving/Dive Shops (SCUBA)

Our location is an awesome one for diving. The coral reef that surrounds us provides opportunities that can only be experienced in few places in the world.

In order to dive, you must be certified to do certain kinds of diving. When you book they will tell you to bring your PADI certification. Don't despair though if you're not certified. Several of the charter businesses provide minimal certification if you take their seven-hour "resort course." That will teach you enough, if you pass, to allow you to go out and do limited diving. Of course, that's an additional charge but worth it to be able to have the experience while you're here.

All of the boats have rates that are adjusted, depending on how much equipment you need. Many serious divers have their own equipment and bring it. Others bring some of their own equipment and most need everything to be provided. Whatever your needs, they'll take care of you.

Most frequently, I use:

**Reef Raiders** at 292-7745
**Captains' Corner** at 296-8865
**Southpoint Dive Shop** at 292-9778

### Do It All!

This is one of the most fun packages and it is exactly what it's called. It is a day of everything. To my knowledge, there is only one company that has a **Do it All!**

You report in at 9:30 and they leave at 10. The day includes waverunners, snorkeling at a wreck, water-skiing, knee boarding, sailing, windsurfing, banana rides, rafts, and kayaks. For additional charge, you can parasail. It also includes a BBQ lunch, veggies and sodas. You end your day at 4. Cost is approximately $100 and about half for children. **Sunset**

**Watersports** is located at the end of William Street at the Historic Key West Seaport (near the Western Union). Ask your concierge or me to make your reservations or you can call them at 296-2554.

## Dolphins

Before you book a dolphin trip, be sure you understand that it is illegal to "swim with dolphins." There are places in the Upper Keys where that experience is available in a controlled environment but it is not possible here. When you book a dolphin trip, there are no guarantees. The captains who run these charters know where to go to see them. Most of the time, they do; sometimes, they don't.

**Wild Dolphin Adventures** at 296-3737
**Wild About Dolphins** at 294-5026
**Dream Catcher Charters** at 305-0497
**Low Key Charters** at 294-3735

## Dry Tortugas National Park/Ft. Jefferson

If you have the time in your trip to take out a full day, this trip is a must! You have 2 choices...boat or seaplane. You leave early in the morning and it takes about 3 hours to get there by boat. Once you're there, you should take the tour of the fort. It is an amazing structure and has an interesting history. You can also go snorkeling around the fort and, if the weather is good, you can choose to take a little side trip to do more diving. The trips are all-inclusive serving breakfast with lunch and snacks on the way back; snorkel equipment and tour of Ft. Jefferson. You get back about 5:30. Both trips are equally good, in my opinion. They're different types of boats.

**Yankee Freedom** at 294-7009
**Sunny Days** at 292-6100
The other choice is to fly. It's more expensive but obviously takes less of your day. It takes 40 minutes to fly each way and you have 2½ hours on the island.

**Seaplanes of Key West** at 294-0709

## Glassbottom Boats

If you don't want to get in the water but want to see some of the reef and fish, the next best thing is a glassbottom boat. Trips last about 2 hours and leave at various times during the day. Both are equal and I have no preference.

**Discovery** at 295-6663

**Pride of Key West** at 296-4527

## Jet Ski/Waverunner/Island Tour

There are many places that rent jet skis and waverunners. You need to understand that you just don't go rent one and then go off on your own. All rental places have courses and you must stay between their markers. Your choice of which place to select will probably be based on where you're staying.

**Key West Water Tours** at 294-6790

**Ski West** at 292-2690

**Holiday Inn Watersports** at 294-2571, Ext. 423

**Sunset Watersports** at 294-1987

One of the most fun ways to jet ski is to take an **Island Tour**. This jet ski tour lasts 2 hours and is a 26-mile tour around the island. During the tour, you can stop and swim if you want. They also have sunset tours for large and small groups.

My daughter's favorite is Key West Water Tours at Hurricane Hole Marina. She says that Jerry, the owner and guide is THE BEST! Ski West and Holiday Inn Watersports both have island jet ski tours as well and I've had satisfied customers there as well.

## Jungle Tours

Fun for the kids...you get to drive little boats. Call **Jungle Tours** at 292-3300.

## Kayak Trips

For those of you who want to get out in the backcountry quietly, a kayak trip might be a good choice for you. Many of the companies will pick you up at your hotel because they often drive to a remote location that you would have difficulty finding if you have a car. Length of tours depends on the company. **Just remember...if the weather has been uncooperative during your stay with too much rain or wind and it has ruined a lot of your activities, you can almost always go kayaking.** If you really enjoy seeing a natural habitat, then a kayak trip can fit your interests. There are many. My favorites are:

**Downwind Kayak Tours** at 797-SAIL(7245)
**Mosquito Coast** at 294-7178
**Outdoor Kayak Adventure** at 295-9898

Many of these trips combine snorkeling and swimming with their trips.


### Parasail

If you've never gone parasailing, GO! I went with my daughter on my 60th birthday...just so I could say "I got high with my daughter on my 60th birthday." You don't even have to wear a bathing suit as you take off from the boat and come down on the boat. They'll ask you if you want them to "dip" you. That means they slow the boat down and you slowly sink into the water and then they rev it back up and up you go. It's your choice. But the whole experience is one like you've probably never come close to. Besides being a beautiful way to get a bird's eye view of the island, it is so quiet and peaceful. I can't encourage you enough to do it. If you do, I doubt that you will regret it. You'll never ever forget the feeling.

**Parawest** at 292-5199
**Sunset Watersports** at 296-2554
**Fury Catamarans** at 294-8899
**Sebago** at 292-2411


### Sailing

One of my favorite sail boats and captains is Capt. Albert Tropea. He's available for charters, short and long, weddings and other customized sails. Call 295-2631 or check the website:

www.keywetsailingadventure.com.

## Snorkel

There are so many snorkel opportunities to choose from and, again, it depends on the kind of experience you want. There are two that are bigger catamarans and carry more people. Between the two, I don't know any difference. I'm sure they would disagree.

**Sebago Catamarans** at 294-5687
**Fury Catamarans** at 294-8899

I usually recommend the smaller boats with a more personal experience. My favorites are:

**Danger Charters** at 296-3272
**Caribbean Spirit** at 296-5556
**Reef Express** at 294-7755
**Seabreeze Snorkel** at 292-7745 (the only one equipped for wheelchairs and a lift to get handicapped people in the water.)
**Stars and Stripes** at 294-7877

## SNUBA

SNUBA is a combination of SNorkeling and scUBA. No dive certification is necessary. It's easy to learn and no prior dive or snorkel experience is necessary. This one's easy; there's only one place:

**SNUBA** at 292-4616

They will pick you up at The Casa Marina, the Reach or The Hilton.

## Combination Trips (My Favorite)

Many of these companies have been mentioned in specific places, but any time I can, I try to convince guests that they need to take one of the combination trips. There are a handful of companies that I think provide an excellent experience.

**Danger Charters** at 296-3272 does a wonderful job with these tours. The larger boat accommodates 18 people. They combine backcountry kayaking and snorkeling. They provide a light lunch and free beer, wine, soda and water as well as all your equipment. Their smaller boat, *Roamer*, goes out in the early afternoon. They also snorkel and kayak as well as go to a pristine island beach. A gourmet lunch is served and they stay out until sunset when they serve a champagne toast. It is always a highlight for those who take it!

Another great combination trip is provided by **Easy Day Charters** at 294-3095. They have two boats, *Easy Day* and *Lucky Day*. Their combination trip involves light tackle fishing as well.

## Sunset Cruises

Very early in the book, I discussed sunset on land. But, there are many, many, many sunset cruises. Nearly every boat offers or would offer some kind of sunset experience. Again, it depends on the kind of experience you're looking for. I am very partial to the beautiful tall ships. They are:

**Schooner Western Union** at 292-1766

**Schooner Liberty** at 292-0332

Other sunset cruises on catamarans and other types of boats are:

**Sebago** at 294-5687 (Combo with snorkeling)

**Seabreeze** at 292-7745 (Combo with snorkeling)

**Fury** at 294-8899 (Combo with snorkeling)

**Stars and Stripes** at 294-7877

## Rum Runners Casino Cruise

No port would be complete without a gambling boat. Rum Runners is "the only game in town." They have day and evening cruises, party cruises and Sunday brunch. It leaves from Hilton Pier. If you have a concierge, ask them. If not, call 295-7775.

Now, you can't say you have no choices of activities involving the water. If you're going to get wet, take towels and hats. Have fun and, again, momma sez, "Don't forget the sunscreen!"

# Chapter 13
# Homes of famous people

**T**his little town has had so many famous people live here that it is truly mind-boggling. You will hear about many of them if you take the trolley or train. Many of them are just "homes" today, not public, and many people don't even realize that someone famous has lived there previously.

Let's start with the most popular houses for touring (alphabetically):

### Audubon House

The Audubon House and Tropical Garden, located at 205 Whitehead Street, is a lovely little escape with a self-guided tour. But, BEWARE, lest you think that it was a home of John James Audubon, famous artist of birds. The owner of the house was Capt. John Geiger who built it in the mid-1800's. Audubon visited Key West before the house was even built and I guess it impressed Geiger, so he named the house after the artist. It is a nice respite and many people get married in the garden. It also has a "ghost" history and is featured on The Ghost Tour.

### Fogarty House

This beautiful house on the corner of Duval and Caroline now is the location for **Fogarty's Restaurant** and the **Flying Monkey Bar**. In 1912, Key West Mayor, Dr. Jeremiah Fogarty, entertained dignitaries here for the opening of the railroad. President William Taft and Henry Flagler were among the dignitaries present. When my daughter worked there, she had an encounter with one of the resident ghosts...in the ladies' room!

### George Carey House/
### Heritage House Museum/
### Robert Frost Cottage

Located at 410 Caroline Street, this elegant old home is open to the public. The garden is also beautiful but the cottage where Robert Frost stayed, when he visited, is also there. The **Orchid Lady tour** starts here as well.

### Hemingway House

Without a doubt, the Hemingway House is the most visited house on the island...and Ernest and one of his wives, Pauline, did live in it. When they acquired it, they renovated it and put in the first swimming pool on the island. The house is located at 907 Whitehead Street. Ask the person selling the ticket if his name is Larry. If so, he's one of the many colorful characters on the island. Tell him Phyllis told you to introduce yourself. It won't help get you a reduced price ticket but you need to meet Larry.

### John Dewey House/Southernmost Motel

John loved his little house at 504 South Street. (It has now become part of Southernmost Resorts.) You know he was an educator and philosopher and, yes, he's responsible for the Dewey Decimal System.

### Oldest House Museum

Some say the Oldest House, at 322 Duval Street, is truly the oldest building in South Florida. Capt. Wallington, his wife and 9 daughters lived there for years.

### Southernmost Mansion

This was originally the J. Vining Harris House and is located at 1400 Duval Street. As I mentioned earlier, the little tour is impressive and admission gives you all day access to the pool and bar.

### Privately Owned Homes

There are also several houses that are not open to the public but it's nice to take a photo from the outside if it's someone who interests you.

### Calvin Klein House

Historically, this really is known as the Richard Peacon house at 712 Eaton Street. Peacon owned the largest grocery store and built this house in the late 1800's. The most famous owner, however, was Calvin Klein. Calvin bought it in 1980 but doesn't own it today.

## Jerry Herman's House

Broadway musician, Jerry Herman, owned the "twin" houses at 701 and 703 Fleming Street. After restoring them, he sold 701 and continued to live at 703 until his partner died.

## Judy Blume's House

Judy and her husband are very active in the community. I'm not going to tell you where they live but I often take my guests to her house, park close by and tell my guests to go stand over in front of "that gate"...quickly. I hurriedly take the photo, we quickly get back in the car and then I tell them whose house it was so they can tell their friends.

I really messed up, however, when my 5th grade school-teacher sister and her family came for a couple of days. I showed them all around but it wasn't until I left them that I realized I had forgotten Judy Blume. When I told her, she actually screamed at me saying, "I can't believe you. I AM A 5TH GRADE TEACHER. Nothing would have impressed my kids more about my entire trip." I sent her a picture later of our niece there. She didn't seem to be impressed...or very forgiving!

## Philip Burton House

Elizabeth Taylor often visited Philip at his home at 608 Angela. Philip himself was interested in Shakespeare and became a playwright and author. As a headmaster of a school, he became the mentor and guardian of Richard Burton. Philip died here 1995.

## Shel Silverstein House

Shel died in 1999. He lived on the west side of the 600 block of Williams Street. Two houses together housed his home and his studio. Until I came here, I only recognized Shel as the author of many of my daughter's favorite books. I had no idea that he was also an artist, cartoonist, and had many very "adult-themed" projects.

### Tennessee Williams' House

Tennessee Williams was a much more prolific writer than Ernest Hemingway and lived here longer but he hasn't had the family to carry on and a house easy for tourists to find. His last house was at 1431 Duncan Street. It has been expanded from the original but it DOES have a tin roof and there's no doubt that it's a HOT TIN ROOF. I always look for the cat on it. It's a private residence now. Next door is the Rose Tattoo. The movie by the same name (adapted from one of Tennessee's plays) was filmed in this house in 1955.

### Thelma Strabel House (the real Southernmost House)

Thelma was a novelist and built her tiny little house at 400 South Street behind a pink wall...or, at least, it's behind a pink wall now. It is THE REAL SOUTHERNMOST HOUSE but there are no signs to tell you that.

It is probably obvious that there are many famous houses in Key West. The absolutely best resource for more information is in **Sharon Wells' Walking and Biking Guide to Key West**. As I mentioned earlier, it is free and available at many locations that distribute newspapers as well as at many of the sites mentioned in her guide.

Tennessee Williams' house

# Chapter 14
# Museums and other
# historic buildings

**S**ome of the houses mentioned in the previous chapter have museums with them and I won't mention them again. Except for The Little White House, the museums mentioned here are not now nor have they ever been homes. They're just museums...that's all...but very interesting!

### Aquarium
In the world of Seaquarium, Sea World and other spectacular aquatic parks, our aquarium pales in comparison. But, in 1934, it was the world's first open air aquarium. It's in the area of Mallory Square.

### Captain Tony's Saloon
The site of Sloppy Joe Russell's original bar is where young Hemingway probably spent too much time. The story goes that the landlord raised the rent and everyone picked up the tables and moved up to the corner location that now houses Sloppy Joe's without missing any business. You might actually find Capt. Tony there.

He's another Key West character and legend in his own time. And, his son was a finalist on one of the early Survivor shows!

### Custom House/Key West Museum of Art and History
This beautiful building was recently renovated and now houses many permanent and temporary exhibits. The building itself is worth the price of admission. It's the big red brick building on Front Street across from Mel Fisher Maritime Museum.

### Flagler Station
At the entrance to Lands End Village on Caroline Street, this little yellow building looks like a train station. It's new but has memorabilia from Henry Flagler and the overseas railroad that he built. Ain't nothing historic about the building!

### La te da
La te da, 1125 Duval Street, is known now for its cabaret, bar,

restaurant and guesthouse but many years ago, Jose Marti, the famous Cuban patriot, revolutionary and martyr made this residence of T. Perez his American headquarters. He made a famous speech standing out on the front balcony that is above the front door. And, how did it get from that historic residence to be called La Te Da? In 1977, it opened as La Terraza de Marti and is now shortened to La Te Da. Go inside to the **By George Bar**. Look at the back wall...they're all original Picassos. THE BEST cabaret shows are upstairs and the By George Bar has some of the island's best piano/vocal entertainment nightly.

### Lighthouse Museum/Keepers Quarters
Across from the Hemingway House at 938 Whitehead Street, this is one of the oldest lighthouses in Florida. There are 88 steps to the top, where the light is still the original. If you make it up there, the view is incredible. Sometimes it's even more so as the Lighthouse Court, a gay men's guesthouse, is next door. Boxing matches used to be held in the yard at the lighthouse and keepers quarters. One of the boxers was often Ernest Hemingway himself.

### Mel Fisher Maritime Museum
Right at the triangle at Front Street and Whitehead is the Mel Fisher Maritime Museum. Mel Fisher spent his life looking for treasures in sunken ships. His famous motto is "Today's the day!" He never gave up and only recently died. His children and business partners still carry on today. The museum houses many of the treasures he did find as well as other maritime exhibits, including boats. His biggest find was the sunken ship "Atocha."

### San Carlos Institute
The San Carlos was built as a political and social gathering place for the many Cubans who lived in Key West. Originally, it was a wooden building but burned. It was rebuilt by the

Cuban Government and reopened in 1924. The Cuban architecture is impressive. The building is open to the public and houses a small museum room. It was built as an Opera House and the theater now hosts a variety of performances.

### Shipwreck Historeum
Did you know that at one time, Key West was **the richest city in the U.S.**? I know it's hard to believe but I kid you not on this fact. And, it was because of all the shipwrecks off shore (lucky they weren't on shore!) and the wreckers who salvaged the loot that made the city so wealthy. With actors, films, laser technology and actual artifacts, they do make "history come alive." Located at the end of Whitehead Street, close to Mallory Square. You can't miss the tower. (It is only fair to tell you that at one time Key West was also the poorest city in the U.S.!)

### Sloppy Joe's Bar
Everyone wants to go to Sloppy Joe's because of the Hemingway influence. So go to the corner of Duval and Greene St., drop in, have a drink and buy a t-shirt. I, personally, would save a dining experience for some of the truly wonderful restaurants that are here but you know you can't miss Sloppy Joe's. It formerly was a bank. The REAL Sloppy Joe's is in the location now occupied by **Capt. Tony's** about a half block down Greene Street toward Whitehead St. Sloppy Joe was a real person...Sloppy Joe Russell and Hemingway spent many hours at that Sloppy Joe's. So, if you want the REAL place, go to Capt. Tony's. There is a lawsuit by Sloppy Joe's against Capt. Tony's over the claim of "first and original" Sloppy Joe's. According to Fast Eddy in the newspaper *Celebrate!*, "Hemingway left to live in Cuba two months before the bar moved to Duval and Greene. He returned 20 years later. He was in disrepute with the locals as to his treatment of his wife and shunned by the town. He NEVER STEPPED FOOT IN THE CURRENT SLOPPY JOE'S, which is now a high-priced tourist trap." Nevertheless, everyone has to do it. When you get

home, no one cares about the truth.

### The Little White House

As a child, I think the first time I ever heard of Key West was because Harry Truman was the first President I was ever aware of and he came here to vacation. The Little White House is located in the area off Whitehead Street, known as Truman Annex. Go figure! You can access it by going to the end of Southard Street, past the guard house and turning right at the first street. Or, if you're in the area at the west end of Front Street, close to the Hilton Hotel, you can walk through the gate and it's right there. The tours are excellent and it is obvious why Truman would find it a relaxing getaway. This was his "Little White House" from 1946-1952. He once said, "I've a notion to move the capital to Key West and just stay."

### Truman Annex

While Truman Annex doesn't fall into any other category, let's just go ahead and talk about it while we're talking about the Little White House.

Truman Annex is now a residential development. It used to be a Navy Base and some of the original buildings have been kept and renovated to become condos. The old weather station building is now part of the Hilton hotel and is a small hotel/guest house called the **Weatherstation Inn**.

Many of the beautiful homes on Whitehead Street were officers' homes. The lighthouse in Truman Annex is now a beautiful private residence.

The **Presidential Gates**, which open to Whitehead Street, were the original gates for the Navy base. They are now only opened for dignitaries.

Truthfully, there is no end to the number of historic buildings as well as homes. Many homes as well as those that are now bed and breakfasts are on the National Historic Register. We are surrounded by history in our buildings.

# Chapter 15
# Artists and Galleries

**V**isual artists abound here. It is truly an artists' colony. Walking from one end of Duval Street to the other will provide opportunities to enjoy several galleries and many different kinds of artists. Some of the galleries house works of individual artists and others house groups of artists. On Duval Street, you will find most of the galleries toward the south end.

In Duval Square, **Jack Baron** has a gallery that's a little off the beaten path. Jack's easily recognizable folk art pieces are examples of "pointillism." That means everything is done with colorful dots.

**Sal Salinero** is another artist who was born in Key West. His works are incredible recreations of nature and wildlife in the tropics. "Realism" is his style. His work is exhibited at the **Gingerbread Square Gallery** at 1207 Duval Street.

Another favorite artist in the area is **Jim Salem**, another realist, who also exhibits at the Gingerbread Square Gallery.

**The Joy Gallery** at 1124 Duval Street features artists **Lucie Bilodeau, Therese Fortin, Thomas M Easley, Irma Quiqley, Jim Trippe, Neva Townsend** and others.

**Alan Maltz Gallery**, 1210 Duval Street, is the place to see Alan's photography, often described as visual poetry, and is one place to buy his books. His book entitled *"Key West Color"* is atop many coffee tables and is a great unbreakable keepsake to take home.

**Luis Sotil** is the "Creator of Naturalismo" and his studio is located at 716 Duval Street. His roosters are outrageous and his distinction is that he only uses natural pigments, instead of paint, to make a statement about the environment. He travels all over the world to collect the unique pigments that are natural products of nature. He has a unique way of expressing his love of nature.

**Wyland** has two galleries on Duval Street. Wyland Galleries of Key West are located at 719 Duval and at 102 Duval. Wyland is famous for his "whaling walls." One was recently done on the side of the Waterfront Market on Caroline Street…not surprisingly on the waterfront.

**Kennedy Studios Gallery** is one of many Kennedy Studios located in colorful destinations. The store has many items for sale besides pictures…and in all price ranges. They have prints and originals and offer a daily $10 special.

A group of local artists have formed their own galleries. The **Island Arts Co-Op** is at 1128 Duval Street, the colorful **Guild Hall Gallery** is at 614 Duval Street and **7 Artists** is at 604 Duval Street.

**The Lemonade Stand** is on the corner of Petronia and Thomas, across from Blue Heaven. **Lettie Nowak** has done portraits of the characters of Key West.

At 606 Greene Street, close to Peppers of Key West, is the **Gallery on Greene**. This gallery houses works of several of the fine artists in town. One of the most famous is **Mario Sanchez**. His works portray early 1900 island life. He carves his pieces and then paints them.

The Gallery on Greene also houses the works of **Joe Loeber**, a renowned German expressionist who now lives and teaches his techniques in Key West.

Next to Gallery on Greene, at 608 Greene Street, is **A Boy and His Dog Fine Art**.

White Street is also home to several galleries that have moved away from Duval. **Barbara Grob's Wave Gallery**, at 1100 White Street, carries her new ART SLUT merchandise. And, all the galleries on White Street are open for a "Walk on White" on the 3rd Thursday evening of each month.

In the world of sculpture, the works of **John Martini**, are exhibited at **Lucky Street Gallery** at 1120 White Street. Abstract steel figures, in color, are his mainstay but he also exhibits prints, drawings and etchings.

One of his most famous works locally, "Where's Jimbo and the Other Giants of the Building Trade?", is hanging at The Green Parrot Bar. Since John lives very close to The Green Parrot, he often went there looking to find some tradesman or specialist in the building trade. Of course, while he was there he had a cool one. This inspired him to create the sculpture that includes Jimbo, the plumber, as well as a carpenter, electrician,

71

lady painter, roofer, and a dog.

It was installed in 1994 and was a day dedicated to the workingmen and women of Key West. For more information, go to http://www.greenparrot.com/martini.

Another popular sculptor is **Helen Harrison**. Her gallery is also on White Street at 835 White Street...**Harrison Gallery**. She has generously allowed one of her pieces, "Cohune Spire" to be located at the Mary Spottswood Park, one of the projects sponsored by the Art in Public Places Board.

**Jeff Beal's** studio is usually open from noon-5 at 933 Fleming Street. Jeff's specialty is colorfully painting antique furniture that he will supply or people provide for him.

**The Haitian Art Gallery**, on the corner of Frances and Southard, has over 5,000 pieces of art and claims to be "the largest collection of Haitian art outside of Haiti."

Other artists use clothing as their medium. One of the most famous designers is **Victoria Lesser**. Her studio, at 1011 Truman Avenue, is the place where Victoria designs fashions for the discriminating consumer who appreciates that the "detailing is what makes the difference between elegance that can be worn and elegance which is merely for show." Most people initially knew of her celebrity when Bill Cosby chose Victoria's pajamas, in cashmere, silk and cotton, but other celebrities include Aerosmith, The BeeGees and Barbara Mandrell.

**Ellen Steininger** is famous for her hand-woven clothing. Ellen owns **Hands On Gallery** at 1206 Duval Street, where her creations are available. And, like Victoria Lesser, she can claim at least one celebrity as a customer. Shirley MacLaine purchased one of her creations.

Under the "doesn't fit any other place" category, stop by and see the **sculpture garden** located between the Waterfront Playhouse and El Meson de Pepe's at Mallory Square. These are unique busts of early Key West leaders. Some people, rather disrespectfully, refer to it as "The Pez Head Garden" but I wouldn't do that.

As I've mentioned, the city sponsored **Art In Public Places**

**Board** is proud of all of the projects that have been commissioned around the city. I mentioned some of them earlier but you will notice them at a variety of locations around the island. One in that general area of Mallory Square is on the wall of Eckerd's. Along with the AIPP Board, the Key West Art and Historical Society and Eckerd's, this project was completed by school children. It is a mosaic in the style of Mario Sanchez.

# Chapter 16
# Entertainment

## Restaurants and Bars

The talented performing artists are also unbelievable. Depending on what you're looking for, you will find extremely talented individuals performing all the time. Most restaurants and bars have live entertainment. Many are local but they often bring the crowd pleasers who seem to be local but who are just here often. Local newspaper advertisements usually list who is performing where and at what time. Venues like Schooner Wharf Bar often have entertainment starting at 10 am and going through the day and night. After being here awhile, everyone has their favorite place and entertainer. They usually go together!

It would be hard to list even my favorites as they change during the seasons. Some performers leave for the summer to go to Provincetown or to Europe to perform.

## Cabaret

**The Crystal Room**, upstairs at La te da, is not to be missed if you enjoy fabulous entertainment. Get there very early. Sitting toward the back is not enjoyable TO ME!

The usual line-up at The Crystal Room are **Randy Roberts**, **Chris Peterson** and **Broadway Three Ways**. (Randy Roberts leaves in the summer.) These are three separate shows. Randy and Chris are each incredible PERFORMERS. They are NOT drag queens. They are female impersonators and do remarkable versions of a variety of female celebrities...Marilyn Monroe, Cher, Joan Rivers, etc. It is a Key West entertainment experience. Broadway Three Ways is three other talented men who change the show each week. During the show, they perform songs from a Broadway musical that changes for each performance. If you enjoy Broadway, check to see if this show is playing on a night you're here.

## Theatres

**The Red Barn Theatre** is located behind the Women's Club on Duval Street. There is a little alley that goes between the

Women's Club and Hard Rock Café that leads back to the little theatre. The season lasts from November until May.

**Regal Cinemas** are located in Sears Shopping Center on N. Roosevelt Blvd. It is a small multiplex.

**San Carlos Institute** on Duval Street has been discussed earlier. It has a small theater, since it was built as an opera house, but it is often used for special functions.

**The Tennessee Williams Theatre** is located on College Drive on Stock Island at Florida Keys Community College. The big productions that happen on the island use that theatre. Tennessee Williams was a friend of the college President and indicated that, when he died, he would leave a legacy for the theatre. With that handshake, the theatre was named after him. Unfortunately, when he died, nothing was left for the theater. Keeping the lights on and the doors open have been especially taxing for the college, especially with budget cuts. Recently a private organization took it over and is hoping to make it succeed. Got any extra money you'd like to donate?

**Tropic Cinema** has just opened at 416 Eaton Street. This building is owned by the Key West Film Society and was recently renovated. The group brings films that often don't make it to our Regal Cinema, for a variety of reasons.

The **Waterfront Playhouse** at Mallory Square is another historic building originally built as fortress style warehouse to store the treasure found in shipwrecks. Their season runs from November to May. In the past, the Waterfront produced many Tennessee Williams plays.

## Music

Would you believe that this town/island has a Symphony and a Pops Orchestra?

The **Key West Pops Orchestra** began 5 years ago and originally donated all of its proceeds to local charities. All together, they gave approximately $125,000 to community organizations. While generous, that could not continue so now they are functioning as any other fundraising board.

The **Key West Symphony** began about the same time. They

bring in outstanding soloists for their concerts and have traveled to Cuba the past three years for a cultural exchange with their symphony.

The **Paradise Big Band** is a smaller group that does not have a board or a season. They play for special events.

The **Island Opera Company** was recently formed; a worthy venue for all of the talented voices that seem to be here.

The **Keys Chorale** is officially a part of Florida Keys Community College. They have their own concerts and sometimes do them with other music organizations. One of the highlights is their Concert under the Stars at Ft. Zachary Taylor in the spring.

**Keys Kids** presents opportunities for children to experience performing at an early age. Many of the talented young people who go on to college in performing arts schools began with Keys Kids.

**Sol Fest** is another program for children, which takes place during the summer. It is a part of the Key West Symphony. At the end of the summer, they produce a musical...the project they have worked on.

**Bahama Village Music Program** offers lessons for underprivileged children. Many talented musicans donate their services to give these children lessons.

# Chapter 17
# Tours

The **Old Town Trolley** and the **Conch Tour Train** were mentioned as a "must do" back in Chapter 6.

There are many bicycle tours but one of the more unique ones is the **Key West Nature Bike Tour**. You can pick it up at Moped Hospital at the corner of Truman and Simonton.

The Original **Ghost Tours** has been featured on ABC, UPN and HGTV. It leaves from the Hotel LaConcha every evening for a 1½ hour walking tour. You don't go in anyplace but hear the story. The creator of Ghost Tours, David Sloan, has written two ghost books about Key West. To me, it's more interesting if you've read the book first but plenty of people don't have that opportunity. You can, of course, buy the book when you sign in. If you want a headstart, go to http://www.phantompress.com. For the Ghost Tour visit http://www.hauntedtours.com or call 294-WALK (9255).

**Key West Pub Crawl** is a 2½ hour walking tour which stops at five different pubs. Your ticket includes a drink at each stop as well as a shirt saying, "The liver is evil...It must be punished!" Ask your concierge or call 305-744-9804.

The Orchid Lady's **Orchid Tour** begins at the **Heritage House** and continues to **Nancy's Secret Garden** and the inner gardens at **Pelican Poop**. Go to http://www.eorchidlady.com or call 877-747-2718.

**"Best of the Bars" Scavenger Hunt** is the "Duval Crawl with a twist." Each participant receives a shirt. Cost is $20 each. Ask your concierge or call 888-222-5148, 305-292-9994 or go to http://www.keywesthunt.com

## The liver is evil...
## It must be punished!

# Chapter 18
# Weddings

**D**estination weddings have recently begun to explode in popularity in locations around the world. The trend is definitely noticeable in Key West and, why wouldn't it? We have the destination without your family having to travel out of the United States. While Key West is costly, it doesn't compare to taking a group further away.

We have such a wealth of wedding locations which are beautiful or unique or both. Most people try to have a wedding at sunset. Some of the favorites locations are:

**Ft. Zachary Taylor State Park**
**Southernmost House**
**Nancy's Secret Garden**
**Hemingway House**
**Audubon House**
**Smathers Beach**
**Key West Butterfly and Nature Conservatory**

There are many boats that can be chartered for a wedding and most large hotels have wedding planners.

Because of the number of weddings being planned to take place here, there are several businesses that specialize in weddings. They can range in price from $100 for a notary to meet you at your specialized location, usually the beach, to much more, depending on how much you want them to plan for/with you. Most offer wedding packages to meet various needs...including me. I'm a Notary and do weddings so give me a call.

# Chapter 19
# Gay Key West

**K**ey West has a reputation for having many gay people. Truthfully, less than 10% of the population are either gay or lesbian but the fact that Key West is such an accepting town allows things to be much more open. Most people in the town (there are always exceptions) value diversity....diversity of color, religion, politics, ethnicity and sexual orientation.

Speaking in generalities, the gay and lesbian population has a high percentage of people who are educated, have professional jobs and money...in addition to a creative, artistic gene that many of us wish we had.

Much of the development in Key West has occurred because gay people began moving here, bought property and renovated it...usually with great style. Many own businesses and are active in all of the organizations in the city. And, they are active in politics. Remember our official city and county motto:

# ONE HUMAN FAMILY

If you haven't lived in an openly gay area, you might not know that the rainbow is a symbol of being gay or of being gay friendly. That's why you see many rainbow flags all over town.

During the month of June, Key West celebrates **PrideFest**. There are many gay pride celebrations held in communities around the world. In 2003, Key West had a celebration that no one could top.

When the original rainbow flag was created by Gilbert Baker, it had 8 colors of the rainbow. Due to printing problems with one of the colors, rainbow flags have only had 7 colors. Movers and shakers in the Key West gay community decided to have a rainbow flag made that went "from sea to shining sea." Gilbert Baker agreed to see that it happened and that the 1.25 mile long flag would include all 8 colors. The plan was for a flag to be designed, sewn and unfurled, during PrideFest, down Duval Street, starting at the Gulf of Mexico and ending at the Atlantic Ocean.

The plan was formed and volunteers from all over the community worked shifts to sew the flag. Needless to say, the project took months to accomplish. When it was finished it weighed 3 tons and was 8000 ft. long and 16 ft. wide. More than 2500 people signed up to line the sides of Duval Street and help unroll it as it moved along. Gay and straight people of all ages, including children, walked for hours in the hot sun to slowly stretch the flag the entire length of Duval Street. For everyone who was involved in the process, who helped sew, fold, unroll or just see it…it was a sight to last a lifetime.

*Photo credit: Roger Cousineau*

In conjunction with the flag, a film was made by Talmadge Heyward, called *Key West: City of Colors*. In early 2004, it was shown at the Sundance Film Festival and has been scheduled in cities around the world. Again, all of us are proud of everything that both of these events show about the spirit of people in this community. For more information, go to http://www.keywestcityofcolors.com For yearly PrideFest information, go to http://www.pridefestkeywest.com

AIDS has taken a huge toll in this community. At the end of White Street, at the beginning of the White Street Pier, is an AIDS Memorial. Key West is the only city in the country that has a city-sponsored AIDS Memorial. Every year a ceremony is held to add more names to the memorial.

Duval Street is somewhat divided with several gay bars clustered together. The block between Angela Street and Petronia Street houses the most in one area.

**Kwest** at 705 Duval Street, has "men only" shows later in the evening but earlier in the evening, it's a very nice friendly place where many locals go and ladies are welcome.

Next door to Kwest is **Aqua**. As you walk past it, you can't help but notice the bar. Doors are wide open and featured pianist, Frank Wood, often plays in the evening. Gay or straight…doesn't matter unless it matters to you.

Across Duval and close to the corner of Petronia Street is the **Bourbon Street Complex**. This is a hub of gay activities. From the bar in front to the garden bar and pool in the back, Bourbon Street is the scene of many special events.

**The 801 Bar**, at the corner of Duval and Petronia, is the place that creates the most buzz for those who aren't used to drag queens. Call them what you will but these guys are entertainers. They have a show every night, upstairs at 801. To get people to go in, they stand outside and talk to people walking down the sidewalk. Honestly, they are very nice people. They don't make their living the way most of us would but that doesn't mean they're not good people. Don't worry…they're not going to molest your children. They're just out there to draw people into the show. I will say truthfully though…don't go to that show if you would be easily offended. It would definitely be X-rated.

When I first moved here and my daughter visited the first time, I showed her around town and we walked the length of Duval Street. That night, however, we went to dinner and when we left, it was dark. As we drove past 801, there were many drag queens standing outside. She got so excited and said, "Look, mom…they come out at night!" Now we can laugh at that since we know many of them. In fact, I've been called "The Fairies' Godmother."

At the end of the island, the quiet end, is South Street…the street with the Southernmost Point. Between Duval and Southard Street is the **Atlantic Shores Resort** and **Diner Shores** (if you're old enough, you'll get it) restaurant. Lots of events take place at Atlantic Shores. On Thursday evenings, they show a relatively new movie outside. Popcorn is available and, of course, the bar is open. Tea Dance takes place every Sunday evening. The pool is clothing optional. Many people who are not gay stay at Atlantic Shores. Whatever floats your boat!

I've mentioned that one of the main things you should do is take the Trolley but there is a **Gay Trolley Ride** on Saturday mornings that begins at 11:00 across from Atlantic Shores. This tour specifically points out the gay history and the influences of that on the city. Anyone, heterosexual or homosexual, can go on the tour but tickets for this specific tour can only be purchased through the Key West Business Guild at 294-4603, the Gay and Lesbian Community Center or Atlantic Shores Resort at 510 South Street.

There are many guesthouses that advertise as being gay but if you are straight and wanted to stay at any of them...you would be welcome. It's your choice.

**BINGO** has never been so much fun as it is on Sunday afternoon. There are now two locations for (Gay) Bingo and they meet at the same time. You have to make a choice. The original one is upstairs at The 801 (corner of Duval and Petronia). The newer one is in the Crystal Room at La te da (1125 Duval). Both start at 5 pm and last until about 7 pm. They both serve pizza. It's lots of fun and many straight people go. All proceeds go to local charities.

**The Key West Business Guild** is similar to a gay chamber of commerce. Monthly luncheons are attended by representatives of all types of businesses. This is one of the most active organizations in the community. For more information, go to http://www.gaykeywestfl.com

**The Gay and Lesbian Community Center** is a place where visitors can get information and where meetings take place. They also have computers for internet access. http://www.glcckeywest.org This website provides a place to purchase the "Sea to Shining Sea" poster. It's a fundraiser for GLCC.

The Business Guild and the GLCC share a building on Truman Avenue, next to Denny's. Parking is an issue. You have a better chance of finding parking close by going south on Duval Street. You can usually find a space with a meter at that end of Duval.

# Part III
# Time to leave

# Chapter 20
# Gifts to take back and shops you might miss

**T-Shirts:** I know it's tempting to take back t-shirts because they're easy to pack and unbreakable but I repeat...be careful which t-shirt shop you go to and be sure to check your receipt to see what you were charged.

I mentioned that Walgreen's, Albertson's and K-Mart all have excellent selections of embroidered t-shirts and other touristy stuff at very reasonable prices. If you have a car, it's definitely worth it to stop there to buy gifts and souvenirs at more reasonable prices.

If you're determined to buy shirts on Duval Street, try a place like **Crazy Shirts**. Their unique shirts are dyed with special things and smell like the color. Some are coffee colored and have that smell; the Key Lime shirts are green and smell like lime. Maybe it doesn't sound too appealing but they're very nice and not like any others. Shirts from establishments are always big hits and will serve as remembrances of your trip for a long time. Favorite shirt places are **Sloppy Joe's, Hog's Breath Saloon, Schooner Wharf Bar, Turtle Kraals, Margaritaville,** and **Blue Heaven**.

Except for The T-Shirt Factory on Simonton, next to Pelican Poop, stores that advertise all kinds of shirts that they will make to order, often with off-color displays hanging in their windows, are the ones to be careful about. I'd just prefer you don't even step inside their door...so don't come running to me if you have a problem.

**Pelican Poop** (mentioned earlier) at 314 Simonton has great Caribbean merchandise. Take the little tour at Pelican Poop. It's an unusual building with an historic background that involves Ernest Hemingway. And, next to Pelican Poop is the T-Shirt Factory. One of the "good," ethical t-shirt stores.

**Key West Aloe** is on the corner of Simonton and Greene Street. They have wonderful aloe products for men and women and dogs. Little gift packages are perfect with variety products and take some home for you as well.

**Kermit's Key West Key Lime Shoppe** is my favorite Key Lime place. You won't believe all of the Key Lime things he has, including lotions. There is tea, salad dressing, cookies, candy, soap…you name it. If it can be made with Key Lime, it's there. One of my favorite items there is Key Lime Pepper. Now that's an easy little bottle to pack! It is so good…I look for things to put pepper on. Of course, there's Key Lime Pie but, as I mentioned earlier, the absolute best treat is Key Lime Pie on a Stick. It's Key Lime Pie, even with Graham Cracker Crust, dipped in Chocolate. Nothing compares. Beware of imitations!

**Key West Hand Print Fabrics** is across from Key West Aloe at the corner of Simonton and Greene Street. If you like fabrics or making quilts, you can get some unique fabrics here.

**Del Sol** is located at 123 Duval Street. It has fun merchandise that I think is especially cute for children or young people you need to buy gifts for. All of their merchandise changes color in the sun. They have special tables that you can put the item on to see how it will change. They have everything from shirts to jewelry to nail polish and on and on…

**Butterfly and Nature Conservatory Gift Shop** has wonderful gifts. Many people have a butterfly artwork display shipped home as they are beautiful and so unique. They also have the Boutique at Clinton Square Market on Front Street with everything butterflies.

**Island Store** at 714 Duval Street is "the home of psychedelic Key West geckos." The selection of island gifts makes it a favorite.

**Mary O'Shea's Glass Garden** is the largest glass studio gallery in the Keys. It's located at 213 Simonton Street.

**Peppers of Key West** is the store on Greene Street with the Pepper Car outside. Take your own beer and go in and taste.

**purplebabydaddies Design Store** features the art of Leslie and Markel Leland. The store features contemporary art, jewelry, leather and other unique gifts. Located at 802 Duval Street, the Lelands like for their shop to be called one of "fun stuff."

You must go by and see **Captain Outrageous** on Caroline Street, between Duval and Simonton. It's a big house and his studio is the porch. He's the one responsible for many of the brightly painted bicycles, scooters and anything else that will hold paint. Captain Outrageous legally changed his name and ran for Mayor once. He's the one who painted my scooter. You can see it on page 94.

**The Conch Tour Train Station** at the corner of Duval and Front Street has Key Lime candy canes. You can't get them anywhere else. They're yummy and easy to pack. (Have them wrap them individually so they don't break.) At the same shop, try a Key Lime Milk Shake. That's not easy to pack but it is very good. Besides, you're on vacation.

**Towels of Key West** has extraordinary towels, robes and slippers, unique and specially made for this store at 806 Duval Street.

**CD's** by your favorite local artist are another way to enjoy Key West for a long time. One of the best sellers is the Caribbean music by One World. Most other local entertainers have their CD's. If you liked them, take them home with you. And, of course, there's Jimmy Buffett.

You can't forget **Baby's Coffee** either. If you're a coffee aficionado, you'll love Baby's. You can get it at Fausto's on Fleming Street or, if you're driving, stop at their shop at MM 16.

**Books:** There are wonderful books about Key West. The "granddaddy" of Key West books is the coffee table book of Key West photos by Alan Maltz called Key West Color. A much smaller book of photos and much less expensive is called Key West. Specialized books about Key West homes, Key West gardens, and other topics are available at many shops, bookstores and guest houses.

And, if you forget something or, when it's time to buy a gift for some occasion, go to http://www.conchtraders.com. If there's someone visiting that you'd like to surprise with a gift, Conch Traders does great baskets and will deliver to their hotel or guest house. Let me know if they can't help. I'll be happy to be your personal shopper.

# Chapter 21
# Have a safe trip

**R**egardless of how you leave, have a safe trip, stay in touch and, most of all, come back. Let me know your suggestions and share good and bad experiences. I told you that I feel personally responsible if someone doesn't have a good trip. I want to do my best to see that it doesn't happen.

As I mentioned before, I am a lowly part timer at a local bed and breakfast…specifically, The Lightbourn Inn at 907 Truman Ave., a 101 year old house. It is listed on The National Historic Register. The next time you come, if you'd like to stay there, call us at 305-296-5152. Check the website first at http://www.lightbourn.com. We have great breakfasts and sometimes, when the bosses are gone, momma does the cooking!

**Y'all come again and tell your friends..only if you had a great trip! If you didn't, you probably didn't listen to Momma so that's not my fault now, is it?**

(And, if you'd like to buy the book, *"Quit Your Job and Move to Key West"* by David Sloan and Chris Schultz, go to http://www.phantompress.com)

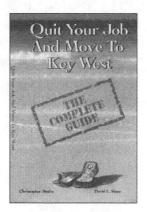

# About Momma

### *Before* Moving to Key West

This was Phyllis May, Ph.D., prior to moving to Key West. Another life...wife, mother, Superintendent of Schools...hair done twice a week, stressed, divorce, daughter off to college, dog put to sleep, mother to assisted living...
RETIRED!

### *After* Moving to Key West

This is Phyllis May after 6 years in Key West. Another life...temp, concierge, student, B&B (sometimes cooking breakfast), fairies' godmother, seminar leader and hopeless volunteer/board member for many non-profit organizations.
REFIRED!

*Photo by Roger Cousineau*

# Index

*Keys To Paradise*

**Things I Want To Do:**

**Restaurants & Bars
I Want To Check Out:**

**Notes:**